YOUR KNOWLEDGE HAS VALUE

- We will publish your bachelor's and master's thesis, essays and papers

- Your own eBook and book - sold worldwide in all relevant shops

- Earn money with each sale

Upload your text at www.GRIN.com
and publish for free

Claudius Benedikt Hildebrand

WindowsMedia - The Role of Microsoft Corporation in the current Multimedia Industry

GRIN Publishing

Bibliographic information published by the German National Library:

The German National Library lists this publication in the National Bibliography; detailed bibliographic data are available on the Internet at http://dnb.dnb.de .

This book is copyright material and must not be copied, reproduced, transferred, distributed, leased, licensed or publicly performed or used in any way except as specifically permitted in writing by the publishers, as allowed under the terms and conditions under which it was purchased or as strictly permitted by applicable copyright law. Any unauthorized distribution or use of this text may be a direct infringement of the author s and publisher s rights and those responsible may be liable in law accordingly.

Imprint:

Copyright © 2002 GRIN Verlag GmbH
Print and binding: Books on Demand GmbH, Norderstedt Germany
ISBN: 978-3-638-63937-8

This book at GRIN:

http://www.grin.com/en/e-book/6346/windowsmedia-the-role-of-microsoft-corpo-ration-in-the-current-multimedia

GRIN - Your knowledge has value

Since its foundation in 1998, GRIN has specialized in publishing academic texts by students, college teachers and other academics as e-book and printed book. The website www.grin.com is an ideal platform for presenting term papers, final papers, scientific essays, dissertations and specialist books.

Visit us on the internet:

http://www.grin.com/

http://www.facebook.com/grincom

http://www.twitter.com/grin_com

UNITEC – INSTITUTE of TECHNOLOGY

Faculty of Business

Department of Information Systems and Computing
Master of Computing Programme

Course ISCG812: Interactive Multimedia Development 1

WindowsMedia

Name: Claudius Benedikt Hildebrand

Due Date: 10. August 2002

Table of Contents

Abbreviations

Codec	compressor/decompressor
DRM	Digital Rights Management
Kbps	Kilobit per second
IT	Information Technology
MP3	MPEG-1, Audio Layer 3
MPEG	Moving Pictures Expert Group
MS	Microsoft
MSN	Microsoft Network
PDA	Personal Digital Assistant
SDK	Software Development Kit
TCP/IP	Transmission Control Protocol / Internet Protocol
WMA	Windows Media Audio
WMV	Windows Media Video

1 Introduction

1.1 What is Multimedia?

Multimedia is one of the buzzwords recently used especially in the new economy. In order to unveil the abstract term "Multimedia", one could come to the conclusion that multimedia "refers to the integration of various forms of information such as text, graphics, sound and images". (Abernethy & Allen, 1999, p. 9)

But in fact, multimedia is more than just combining several types of media. Information technology offers the possibility of adding interactivity between the user and the media. A TV channel is not regarded as a multimedia application because of the lack of interactivity although different types of media are used simultaneously. Nevertheless, clicking through a digital encyclopaedia having sound and images in it, is seen as stand-alone multimedia. The next step in the multimedia development stage distributed multimedia. Multimedia elements are no longer stored locally on a CD-ROM as we have seen in the stand-alone multimedia example. They are remotely stored on servers being connected via a network and therefore can be accessed from anywhere in the world. (Agnew & Kellerman, 1996)

1.2 Microsoft, the leading Multimedia Company?

Microsoft Corporation is one of the global players in the software development market. As more than 85% of all client PC operating systems being sold are Microsoft products (Miles, 2000) it is worth to discover the efforts Microsoft made in the multimedia sector. Within any recent Microsoft operating system, there is an application included to enable people to playing multimedia files.

Everything began in fall 1991 with the release of Media Player for Windows 3.0 shortly after the first PC soundcard was available. The development continued and by time, more and more features have been added until October 2001, Windows Media Player for Windows XP was released. (Microsoft Corporation, 2002a)

In September 2002, the next version of the Windows Media Series 9, code-named Corona, will be launched including several new features which will be presented later on in this assignment. (Microsoft Corporation, 2002b)

1.3 Procedure and Analysis Objectives

This report will evaluate the role of Microsoft Corporation in the current multimedia industry. In order to get an impression about Microsoft's business, there is an overview of Microsoft's products and services at first. Next, it will be Microsoft's strongest competitors in the operating system market as most consumers of multimedia services have a Windows operating system which included a player for multimedia content. This player called Windows Media Player is being discussed and compared to the RealNetworks' RealOne player which is regarded as one of Microsoft's strongest competitors in the multimedia business. Consecutively, there is an investigation of electronic devices currently supporting the technology provided by Microsoft including different audio- and video codecs. Finally, there is a conclusion showing the results of the research and giving some recommendations when deciding which multimedia environment to choose: Microsoft or RealNetworks.

2 Key features of the Multimedia Industry

2.1 Microsoft's main business activities

Microsoft Corporation was founded in 1975 by William H. (called Bill) Gates and Paul Allen. In 1981 they started programming operating Systems for IBM PCs because IBM thought programming operating systems would not make any profit. The first version of Windows with graphical desktop and mouse support was released in 1985. (Microsoft Corporation, 2002d)

The development continued and the formerly garage based company turned into a global stock-listed enterprise employing around 50.000 people worldwide and having had a revenue of more than 28 billion US$ in the fiscal year ending June 30th, 2002. (Microsoft Corporation, 2002c)

The products and services offered by Microsoft do not only include operating systems, but range from obvious ones like selling software development tools, server environments, office applications and multimedia services in the internet up to holiday offers (Expedia) and financial services (MoneyCentral).

Microsoft themselves divides its business activities currently on their website into seven categories:

- **Windows**

  Client operating systems, e.g. Windows2000, WindowsME, WindowsXP and technologies e.g. Windows Media, Internet Explorer, DirectX

- **Office**

  Productivity tools, e.g. MS Word, MS Excel, MS Powerpoint

- **Servers**

  Server software for multiple purposes, e.g. databases, portal systems, mail management

- **Developer Tools**

  Software development tools for programming applications in the Windows environment, e.g. Visual Studio

- **Games and X-Box**

  Games for Windows operating systems, game console X-Box and gaming hardware, e.g. Sidewinder Gamepad

- **MSN Services**

  Portal for several internet based services incl. emailing, stock quotes, internet access, gaming and music

- **Business Solutions**

  All-in-one software solutions for small and medium sized businesses

2.2 Microsoft's competitors

Microsoft as a diversified company doing its business in many different industries, is faced a couple of competitors. The focus in this assignment will be held on the competitors being primarily active in the multimedia area.

Concerning the Windows client operating system, Microsoft is leading with a market share of almost 90%. Competing operating systems like Linux or

3

MacOS lead to shadowy existence on desktop computers. (Miles, 2000) The very high level of distribution and market share is Microsoft's unique point. It enables their products to become de-facto standards. This could not the achieved by products of other software vendors as their market share is much smaller. This issue is discussed controversy in the media whether Microsoft abused its market power to distort competition or not.

Nevertheless, in regard to the server market, Microsoft is namely market leader with 41% market share in 2000, but Linux with a constantly growing market share of currently 27% is regarded as the strongest competitor (Shankland, 2001). This is very important as the server system environment for providing multimedia content can differ from the client's software environment.

In regard to the multimedia player applications which are explained in great detail in the third chapter, there is a three-event competition between Windows Media Player provided free of charge by Microsoft bundled with the operating system, RealOne Player built by RealNetworks and revived QuickTime by Apple which are both beard to charge. (Olsen, 2002) The market share of Windows Media Player and RealOne are close to each other, whereas QuickTime is behind. An in-dept investigation of the respective market shares and a comparison of the features among Windows Media Player and RealOne as its strongest competitor are available in chapter 3.2 of this assignment.

2.3 Microsoft's effort in the Multimedia Industry

Half a year after the development of soundcards for PCs in 1991, Microsoft offered so-called 'Multimedia Extensions' for their in these days current Windows 3.0 operating system to enable users listening to audio files and music CDs. A slightly enhanced version of the 'Media Player' was standard in Windows 3.1 which was launched April 1992.

End of 1994, Windows95 was set public with a more powerful version of the 'Media Player' making use of the newly implemented 32-Bit functionality. Furthermore, using different codecs and filters for video and audio streams was possible.

WindowsME and Windows2000 operating systems have been equipped with newer versions of the 'Windows Media Player', too. The most important new features have been the integration of support for networks in order so allow streaming multimedia content and the addition of tools to manage and create audio/video content.

The up-to-date version of Windows Media Player was shipped together with the release of WindowsXP in October 2001. It offers support for watching DVD videos and burning audio files directly on a CD. (Microsoft Corporation, 2002a)

In this release, Microsoft has included its own codecs for audio and video content. This lead to severe trouble, as open standards have been faded into the background and competitors like RealNetworks brought Microsoft to court. (Wilcox, 2002)

In September 2002, Microsoft will announce Windows Media Series 9, a new package of software applications used to create, distribute and enjoy multimedia content. (Microsoft Corporation, 2002b)

Having seen this timeline, Microsoft has played an important role in the multimedia industry. Currently, the Windows Digital Media department is headed by David Britton, who will continue Microsoft's efforts of building a package of applications covering the entire value chain. Windows Media 9 Series, which is being explained in chapter 3.3, will be the cutting edge software package offered by Microsoft for multimedia development. The question of whether to follow open standards or to rely on proprietary standards can be seen in different ways and has to be discussed later on in this assignment.

3 Current software applications used in the Multimedia Industry

3.1 Windows Media Series

Windows Media Series is a package of tools to provide users with the capabilities to capture, convert, distribute and play multimedia content.

3.1.1 Windows Media Encoder

Windows Media Encoder is used to capture and convert multimedia content from several sources. There are three major usages:

a)   Capture from existing video files

If a multimedia file has been created by another application, it can be opened and converted into a format which can be streamed over a network.

b)   Capture from desktop

Especially in an educational context, capturing from the full screen or just certain windows can be helpful to show how to perform certain steps on a computer. In e-learning environments, computing courses are often held this way.

c)   Capture from web cam or TV-card

Live video being digitalized by a web cam or TV-card can be saved and converted using Windows Media Encoder. The content delivery process takes place either from a saved file or by capturing content in real-time.

Windows Media Encoder has the capability to broadcast content to 50 clients simultaneously over a network. For higher volumes of connections and higher performance in streaming media, Windows Media Services combined with a Windows2000 Server environment is required. (Microsoft Corporation, 2002h)

3.1.2 Windows Media Services

Windows Media Services offers the possibility to broadcast a large number of multimedia streams over a network. In contrast to a web-server, Windows Media Services measure bandwidth usage during the streaming process and send data in a continuous flow, whereas web-servers are optimized for delivering large amounts of data in huge bursts. During the development process, the focus was being held on scalability, reliability, high quality of delivered content and financial issues. That's why Windows Media Services has been completely integrated into Microsoft's current Windows2000 Server environment without the need for purchasing additional licenses.

An independent test by ZD Labs (2000) verified the performance and scalability of Windows Media Services. In a first test, 22kbps narrowband video stream had been served simultaneously to more than 9000 clients without dropping streams. A second test serving 100kbps broadband video streams proofed smooth playback on more than 2400 concurrent clients and an accuracy of

99,9999999% of delivered packets in a 14-day test with an endless loop of the above mentioned 100kbps video stream; a very impressive performance!

3.1.3 Windows Media Player

Microsoft offers several versions of its current Windows Media Player. The most recent one for MS Windows operating system is called Windows Media Player for WindowsXP. Unfortunately, this version (Windows Media Player 8.0) is only available for users having WindowsXP as their operating system. Other users have to take the older 7.1 release which lacks several features.

Besides players running in a Windows operating system environment, there are distributions of the Windows Media Player for MacOS, Sun Solaris, several handheld-PCs and portable music devices.

In the area of audio and video there are many new features being available for users of the Windows Media Player for XP:

Audio: Audio-CDs can now be ripped directly onto the hard disk without the use of any third-party product. The audio files being created are using the Windows Media Audio 8 codec which offers nearby CD-quality but needs only half as much storage as the popular MP3 format.

ID3v2, a very common standard for adding song titles, artist and album information to MP3 audio files is now fully supported.

Audio-CDs can now be burnt directly from files being on the user's hard disk without using third party products. The writing-speed is not limited to single speed but can use the full speed which is available by the CD-writer.

Windows XP themes are supported and new visual styles coming up when playing music have been added.

Video: DVD videos are now fully supported and can be watched without using any third party player software. In full screen mode, the control buttons are easier to access now than in previous versions. Navigating though the DVD has been made easier by showing chapter titles and not only play-list numbers. Additional DVD information and chapter titles are now stored for later offline reading.

Digital video content can be transferred to handheld PC devices as easy as transferring audio content.

In addition to the new features in the audio and video sector, there are three more ground-breaking features to mention:

Intelligent Media Management keeps track of the users' audio/video files. Even if files are moved to another directory, play lists need not be rebuilt.

Player Management allows creating customized versions of the Windows Media Player and skins which can enhance productivity within companies by providing targeted features.

Auto play functionality has been enhanced so when inserting an Audio-CD or a DVD, a prompt appears asking whether to start playback or offering other possibilities. Even when connecting a digital camcorder to the PC, auto play functionality starts and asks the user what he wants to do with the device attached. (Microsoft Corporation, 2002i)

Offering a large number of features and being available free of charge with any purchase of the MS WindowsXP operating system it seems to be a very difficult market for competitors. In addition, the spread of Microsoft's Windows Media Player is pretty high because it is bundled with the operating system whereas competitors have to convince potential customers that their product is superior in order to have them download and install it.

3.1.4 Windows Media Rights Manager

Especially multimedia content providers in the internet will love the DRM features provided by Windows Media Services. They offer the possibility to secure copyright demands in digital media. Digital media files are equipped with a unique license key that is bound to one specific computer. In case of copyright infringements, officials can easily discover the person who breached the copyright. Furthermore, different licensing models and high spread of the playback application combined with revocation of out-of-date players make DRM an indispensable tool for every distributed multimedia provider. (Microsoft Corporation, 2002f)

3.1.5 Windows Media SDK

Hardware and software developers planning to use Windows Media content in their devices can use the Windows Media SDK which will provide them with ready-to-use components for their applications. Software developers find bits of software which can easily be integrated into their applications offering high performance and security without the hassle of programming everything from scratch whereas hardware manufacturers get information of how to use Windows Media Services in embedded systems. (Microsoft Corporation, 2002g)

3.2 Comparison – Windows Media Player vs. RealOne

Windows Media Player and Real One, formerly known as Real Player, face head-to-head competition according to a research by Gartner Group in July 2001. This investigation discovered that 12% of all American adults use Windows Media Player at least once a week while another 12% use Real Player. (Hicks, 2001)

Comparing the market share of both players at home or at work shows, that Windows Media Player has a 63% market share at workspaces whereas RealOne has only 60%. It is the different way around at the market share on home PCs where RealOne leads having 60% spread in front of Windows Media Player with only 53%. (Olsen, 2002) Numbers add up to more than 100% because Windows Media Player as well as RealOne could be installed on a single PC.

As both players basically provide access to multimedia content, it will be the additional features that make the difference. Following, there is a feature comparison between Windows Media Player for Windows XP and RealOne:

Installation: Windows Media Player for Windows XP is bundled with the operating system. Therefore, no software installation has to be performed by the customer. RealOne is a third party application not being shipped together with the operating system. Users are forced to install the software in order to use it. Finding the free trial-version on the RealNetworks website could be difficult as the layout is a bit confusing (Chandler 2002).

Costs: Windows Media Player for Windows XP is purchased together with the operating system. Costs are only caused by optional third-party applications. RealOne instead comes as a 14-day trial version. If the software is used after the trial period, a monthly fee of 9,95US$ has to be paid. In case, a user already has to pay loads of money for internet access, it could be possible that he won't spend money on RealOne as he gets a similar product by Microsoft free of charge.

Codecs: Both players support a wide range of codecs for audio and video playback. Nevertheless, in some cases, a codec is not available and has to be downloaded separately. WMA/WMV is the preferred codec by Windows Media Player whereas RealOne supports a larger number of codecs, especially RealAudio/RealVideo. (RealNetworks, 2002a)

DVD: Windows Media Player for Windows XP is able to play DVDs instantly, whereas RealOne doesn't support it.

CD-Writing: Windows Media Player for Windows XP has native support for many CD-Writers and can burn audio files directly onto the CD without using any third party product. Moreover, the speed of writing CDs is only limited by the speed of the CD-Writer. RealOne needs a special Plug-in to write CDs. Speed is limited to double-speed only, so writing a 74minute long Audio-CD will take 37 minutes.

Content: Having special agreements with many content providers (e.g. CNN, ABCNews, FOXSports.com, NBA.com, NASCAR.com, Wall Street Journal, C/NET, Animal Channel and many more) RealOne users seem to have an advantage compared to users of Windows Media Player.

Privacy: There are many discussions whether Microsoft gathers private information from users of the Windows Media Player. In a recent bug fix for the application, Microsoft claimed the right to access a user's PC and manipulate it. (Curtis & Mueller, 2002) In regard to the activation policy when installing MS Windows XP operating systems, this could be an issue of fear for customers in regard to their privacy.

Security: Microsoft operating systems are proofed to have several security holes which are being fixed using service packs and bug fixes. As Windows Media Server and Windows Media Player are completely integrated into the operating system, problems concerning the overall security can arise. RealOne is aware of this problem and discovers security as one competitive advantage which has to be defended.

Server: When looking at the players for multimedia content, it is vital to have at least a short look to the background, the server that continuously feeds the player with content. The key findings of a comparison figured out, that Windows Media Services is less costly than RealSystem 8 due to the integration of Windows Media Services into Windows Server operating system. The encoding engine of Windows Media Services discovered to be easier to administrate, offer a higher performance and comes with several useful features in comparison to RealSystem Producer. (Approach Inc., 2001) Furthermore, to ensure easy configuration and high scalability, Windows Media Services are preferred than RealSystem.

Microsoft planning to release Corona in short future and RealNetworks recently having released the new server platform Helix Universal Server are currently improving the performance of their server environment. According to a research by RealNetworks (2002a), Helix Universal Server will be twice as fast as Corona, support even more codecs (Corona 13, Helix Universal Server 27) and be running in 14 operating system environments whereas Corona will only be available for Windows2000 Server.

3.3 Windows Media Series 9 – Corona

Microsoft will introduce the new Windows Media Series 9 Beta code-named Corona to the public on September 4th, 2002. Corona is supposed to

11

revolutionize the digital media market according to Microsoft's expectations. Indeed, there are several improvements, on the one hand for end customers and on the other hand for content developers.

End consumers will regard the "instant-on" and "always-on" functionality as major improvements, as the streaming process has been optimized and therefore congestion will belong to the past. To achieve this goal, buffering which had caused several delays, had been shortened.

In addition to that, Windows Media Series 9 including the new WMA Codec Version 9 is the first application enabling 6-channel surround sound in extraordinary high quality being broadcasted via TCP/IP network environments. Furthermore, WMV Codec Version 9 has been improved and will be able to serve higher video quality than before.

Content developers can make use of Corona's new plug-in model which allows easy integration of multimedia content into other application using an improved SDK. Besides, Corona's new compression techniques will result in almost twice as many streams per server compared to Windows Media Services and lower bandwidth usage leading to lower costs per stream. The capability of adding advertisements dynamically to multimedia content will offer new ways and business models to content providers. (Microsoft Corporation, 2002j)

Having seen the announced features of Microsoft's new Windows Media Series 9, one may not forget that the version which is launched in September 2002 is still in Beta state. A definite release date for the final public is not yet known.

4 Current technologies used

4.1 Supported Software/Hardware Platforms

Windows Media Player is available in different versions for every Windows operating system running on a PC. The most recent version, Windows Media Player for WindowsXP is only available for users having installed Windows XP (Home or Professional) as their operating system. Even for old, almost out-fashioned operating systems like Windows95 or WindowsNT, which are bit by bit replaced with Windows98/WindowsME or Windows2000, there is a version of Windows Media Player available, offering at least basic multimedia playback functionality. (Microsoft Corporation, 2002l)

Users of MacOS or Solaris do not have to abandon using Windows Media Player. There are specialized versions of the application for these operating systems having adapted the look-and-feel people are used to. Nevertheless, these versions do not offer the same amount of features and functionality, as the version optimized for Windows offers. (Microsoft Corporation, 2002k) The main purpose of these versions is not to exclude users with a different operating system than Windows from using Windows Media optimized content. The ulterior motive is that in short future, people could have to pay for content and Microsoft wished to have a huge number of users preferring their software in order to convince Content Providers of using Windows Media Series as their content delivery platform or to produce content by themselves.

Windows Media Player is also available for Pocket-PCs, Palm-size PCs, Handheld-PCs and digital music devices but the functionality is limited due to lower processor power, fewer memory and smaller screens in comparison to desktop computers or high performance notebooks.

4.2 Portable Devices

According to Metcalf's law, the user's benefit of taking part in a network with n participants is n^2 in concern to several consumer goods. (Baldi, 2002) Microsoft must have adopted this idea when signing up contracts with manufacturers of portable music devices such as CD- and MP3 players, car/home stereo producers and PDA makers. Furthermore, music can be transmitted wireless to playback devices and MS X-Box, the new gaming console, has built-in support for Windows Media content. (Microsoft Corporation, 2002m)

The more devices support Windows Media the more useful the technology is for the consumers, as they can easily share and distribute content among these devices. Microsoft's aim is to provide an all-in-one solution to enable users doing everything in regard to multimedia content without the need for third-party products. Having signed up contracts with major hardware vendors (e.g. Cirrus Logic, ESS Technologies, NEC, Sanyo, Toshiba), there are more than 120 different products directly supporting Windows Media right now. Over 27 million devices being shipped in 2002 will support the new technology. (Microsoft Corporation, 2002n)

4.3 Windows Media 8 Codec vs RealMedia 8 Codec

In order to deliver high-quality content to the user, Microsoft and RealNetworks have developed specialized codecs for audio and video compression. The main purpose of a codec is to compress data. Compressed data needs less bandwidth and enables users with slow modem connections access to multimedia services.

Microsoft developed the WMA8 codec for audio compression which allows music in CD quality being delivered at 64kbps. WMV8 can broadcast video content using a bit rate of 500kbps, which offers an almost similar quality than a DVD movie. In comparison to the former version 7 of the WMV codec, a 30% reduction in bandwidth usage has been achieved without any significant loss in quality.

RealNetworks RealAudio8 codec can deliver CD quality music at 128kbps, which is twice as much as WMA8 needs. To broadcast a video in high quality, a bit rate of 750kbps is necessary, which is 50% more than required by WMV8. (Approach Inc., 2001)

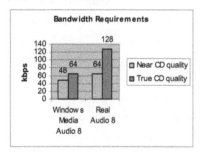
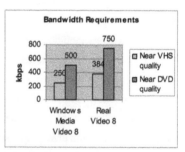

Needing less bandwidth while offering a similar or even better quality of content, the WindowsMedia codec technology used by Microsoft seems to perform better than RealNetworks RealMedia codec. Nevertheless, the overall performance of a broadcasting multimedia server environment depends on various components, so judging that WindowsMedia in general was superior to RealNetworks just in regard to the codecs would be wrong.

14

4.4 Open vs. proprietary standards

Having seen in the previous chapter that Microsoft as well as RealNetworks has introduced its own proprietary standard for audio and video compression, it is surprising that there is a third, open standard called MPEG-4.

MPEG-4 is the advancement of the open standards MPEG-1 and MPEG-2 which were used to deliver standardized digital audio/video content on Video CDs and later on also in digital TV receivers or on DVDs. It contains a set of technologies to enable smooth broadcast of multimedia content in networked environments similar to the existing ones by Microsoft and RealNetworks. The new thing about MPEG-4 technology is the integration of interactive elements. Especially in the field of e-commerce, many new business models are emerging. (Borland, 2001) According to the definition of multimedia in the first chapter, the last missing bit of the puzzle, *interactivity*, will complete the overall picture.

Making use of state-of-the-art audio and video compression technologies and maintaining a very high level of quality as introduced by DVDs, the range of MPEG4's usage is widely spread. The integration of DRM tools and an object-oriented programming language make it a real alternative to the existing products. Especially for wireless services where bandwidth has to be shared with other users, MPEG-4 offers a 30% higher compression rate than MP3 which is commonly used for audio compression. In addition to that, powerful error compression algorithms have been implemented. (iVast, 2002) That's why MPEG-4 could be at least an alternative for cable and telephone companies that do not want to be locked to one manufacturer's standard rather than for a mass market. Microsoft and RealNetworks as the two biggest players in the distributed multimedia business currently stick to their own standards even though Microsoft themselves had been working on the development of MPEG-4 in the early stages. Fortunately MPEG-4 playback is supported in the current versions of Windows Media Player and RealOne. (Borland, 2001) However, only the Helix Universal Server will support serving the new format. Neither Windows Media Services nor Corona will be able to perform this task. (RealNetworks, 2002)

5 Conclusion

Since fall 1991, by releasing a Media Player for Windows 3.0, Microsoft is working in the multimedia business. During the following years, the application has been continuously improved and new features were added. Finally, Windows Media came up as a set of tools assisting users in creating, distributing and playing multimedia content. The most important application in this package is the so called Windows Media Player.

Windows Media Player for WindowsXP is Microsoft's current multimedia player . It has loads of features, which nobody dared to think of when the first media player had been released. Many of these features are only needed by so-called 'power-users' and lots of people never use them. Due to RealNetworks, Microsoft's strongest competitor in the distributed multimedia industry, there was a head-to-hear race who offers the best player. There have been many comparisons between the respective features each player offers but basically they do the same thing: playback of multimedia content.

Due to Microsoft's business strategy of shipping the Windows Media Player together with the Windows operating system, the player has a large market share. RealNetworks cited Microsoft before the court. They claimed Microsoft has abused its market power by bundling the player with the operating system. Nevertheless, RealOne which is the multimedia player provided by RealNetworks has a similar market share even though people had to download the application and install it manually. As installing an application could be a bit difficult especially for inexperienced users. In comparison to Windows Media Player, RealOne is not available free of charge. There is a free trial period but afterwards, a monthly fee has to be paid. This leads to the conclusion that there might be a competitive advantage for Microsoft's Windows Media Player.

Having a look on the server environment, it is similar. Content providers using Windows2000 as their server operating system can use Windows Media Services without any additional cost. Research (see chapter 3) discovered, that Windows Media Services are easier to configure than RealNetwork's new release of the Helix Universal Server which requires the purchase of licenses for streaming multimedia content. Anyway, the free choice of the server operating system and the support for tons of different multimedia codecs make

Helix Universal Server a real alternative to Windows Media Services. Scalability is very important when providing multimedia content as the demand for high quality content is rising. RealNetworks claims that Helix Universal Server can serve almost two times more streams simultaneously as Windows Media Services' successor, the upcoming Corona can serve. If this pronouncement emerges to be true, Helix Universal Server should be the preferred server software. In contrast to Windows Media Services or Corona which can only serve content encoded in a proprietary Microsoft codec, Helix Universal Server will not only serve RealNetworks encoded content, but it will also support WMA/WMV and others.

Having spoken about a suitable codec, one has to remember that MPEG-4 combines several advantages and does not lock a content provider to the proprietary standards of one multimedia company. Helix Universal Server has built-in support to serve MPEG-4 content. Fortunately, either RealOne or Windows Media Player support playing it. Perhaps, not sticking to proprietary standards and using open standards will be the silver bullet in content delivery.

For multimedia content providers the question arises, whether using Microsoft's or RealNetworks' products to broadcast the content. According to the findings in this assignment, the best solution seems to be having Helix Universal Server running in a Linux operating system environment due to its high performance. The preferred codec is MPEG-4 as it offers the possibility of paying for content and e-commerce. MPEG-4 offers high content quality by using less bandwidth than other codecs and content provider do not run the risk of being locked to proprietary standards. As Windows Media Player is bundled with the Windows operating system, it has a large market share and therefore will be the preferred player for multimedia content. Another aspect one has to consider is that Windows Media Player does not require monthly fees to be paid.

Unfortunately, there is no all-in-one solution available from one software developer satisfying all needs. But the combination which is presented here should not cause any major problems and combine the advantages of each single technology used to ensure further development in the multimedia business with lots of new applications and content.

6 References

Abernethy, K., & Allen, T. (1999): *Exploring the digital domain: An introduction to computing with multimedia and networking*. Brooks/Cole Publishing Company

Agnew, P. W., & Kellerman, A. S. (1996): *Distributed multimedia: Technologies, applications, and opportunities in the digital information industry*. New York: ACM Press

Approach Inc. (2001): *Microsoft Windows Media Services and RealNetworks RealSystem: Feature Comparison*. Retrieved August 04, 2002 from URL: http://www.approach.com/digitalmedia/docdetails.asp?doc=WM%2DRN+Comp arison%2Exml&dl=1

Baldi, S. (2002): *E-Business: Concepts and applications: Information goods*. Retrieved August 04, 2002 from URL: http://www.ebs.de/Lehrstuehle/Wirtschaftsinformatik/NEW/Courses/Semester4/ E-Bus/02%20Information%20Goods.pdf

Borland, J. (2001): *MPEG-4's features: Feasible or too sci-fi?* Retrieved August 04, 2002, from URL: http://news.com.com/2100-1023-271255.html

Chandler, N. (2002): *Media player madness: Streaming kings rumble for the multimedia title belt*. Retrieved August 04, 2002 from URL: http://www.smartcomputing.com/editorial/article.asp?article=articles/2002/s1304 /04s04/04s04.asp

Curtis, J. & Mueller, D. (2002): *Media Player-Patch mit Spionage-Software*. Retrieved August 04, 2002 from URL: http://news.zdnet.de/story/0,,t101- s2118270,00.html

Hicks, T. A., gartner.com (2001): *RealNetworks Still Neck and Neck With Microsoft for Media Players*. Retrieved August 04, 2002 from URL: http://www4.gartner.com/resources/101300/101343/101343.pdf

INT Media Group (2002), *codec – webopedia.com*. Retrieved August 04, 2002, from URL: http://www.webopedia.com/TERM/c/codec.html

iVast (2002), *About MPEG4*. Retrieved August 04, 2002, from URL: http://www.ivast.com/aboutmpeg4/

Microsoft Corporation (2002a), *Digital Media Timeline in Windows*. Retrieved August 04, 2002 from URL:
http://www.microsoft.com/windows/windowsmedia/press/dmtimeline.asp

Microsoft Corporation (2002b), *Windows Media 9 Series Tech Summit*. Retrieved August 04, 2002 from URL:
http://www.microsoft.com/windows/windowsmedia/events/wmsummit/

Microsoft Corporation (2002c), *About Microsoft*. Retrieved August 04, 2002 from URL: http://www.microsoft.com/presspass/inside_ms.asp

Microsoft Corporation (2002d), *Fast facts*. Retrieved August 04, 2002 from URL: http://www.microsoft.com/museum/FastFacts098-94354.doc

Microsoft Corporation (2002e), *Windows Media Services 4.1*. Retrieved August 04, 2002 from URL:
http://www.microsoft.com/windows/windowsmedia/technologies/services.asp

Microsoft Corporation (2002f), *Features of DRM*. Retrieved August 04, 2002 from URL:
http://www.microsoft.com/windows/windowsmedia/wm7/drm/features.asp

Microsoft Corporation (2002g), *Application Development*. Retrieved August 04, 2002 from URL:

http://www.microsoft.com/windows/windowsmedia/create/develop.asp

Microsoft Corporation (2002h), *Windows Media Encoder: Whitepaper*. Retrieved August 04, 2002 from URL:
http://download.microsoft.com/download/winmediatech40/Update/2/W98NT42K MeXP/EN-US/Encoder_print.exe

Microsoft Corporation (2002i), *What's new in Windows Media Player for Windows XP*. Retrieved August 04, 2002 from URL:
http://www.microsoft.com/windows/windowsmedia/windowsxp/whatsnew.asp

Microsoft Corporation (2002j), *Windows Media 9 Series*. Retrieved August 04, 2002 from URL:
http://www.microsoft.com/windows/windowsmedia/9series/default.asp

Microsoft Corporation (2002k), *Windows Media Player for Mac OS X*. Retrieved August 04, 2002 from URL:
http://www.microsoft.com/windows/windowsmedia/software/Macintosh/osx/defa ult.asp

Microsoft Corporation (2002l), *Players*. Retrieved August 04, 2002 from URL:
http://www.microsoft.com/windows/windowsmedia/players.asp

Microsoft Corporation (2002m), *Portable devices*. Retrieved August 04, 2002 from URL: http://windowsmedia.com/mg/portabledevices.asp

Microsoft Corporation (2002n), *Windows Media Consumer Electronics Leadership Fact Sheet*. Retrieved August 04, 2002 from URL:
http://download.microsoft.com/download/winmediatech40/fs/1.0/W9X2KMeXP/E N-US/ConsumerElectronics.exe

Miles, S. (2000), *Linux closing in on Microsoft market share, study says.* Retrieved August 04, 2002, from URL: http://news.com.com/2100-1001-243527.html?legacy=cnet

Olsen, S. (2002), *Statistics firms revisit QuickTime counts.* Retrieved August 04, 2002, from URL: http://news.com.com/2100-1023-937302.html?tag=rn

RealNetworks (2002), *RealNetworks competitive advantage.* Retrieved August 04, 2002, from URL:
http://www.realnetworks.com/solutions/leadership/advantage.html

Shankland, S. (2001), *Linux growth underscores threat to Microsoft.* Retrieved August 04, 2002, from URL: http://news.com.com/2100-1001-253320.html?legacy=cnet

Wilcox, J. (2002), *Digital media: Will Microsoft win again?* Retrieved August 04, 2002, from URL: http://news.com.com/2100-1023-938997.html?tag=rn

ZD Labs (2000), *Windows Media Server: Unicast streaming test.* Retrieved August 04, 2002, from URL: http://etestinglabs.com/main/reports/msstream.pdf

www.ingramcontent.com/pod-product-compliance
Lightning Source LLC
LaVergne TN
LVHW042128070326
832902LV00037B/1462